WASTE DISPOSAL

Sally Morgan

W
FRANKLIN WATTS
A Division of Grolier Publishing
NEW YORK • LONDON • HONG KONG • SYDNEY
DANBURY, CONNECTICUT

Picture Credits:

Tony Stone Images: cover main image (Jeremy Walker) and pages 4 (Jeremy Walker), 8 (Jay. S. Simon), 9 bottom (David Woodfall), 12 (John Edwards), 13 top (Hans Peter Merten), 14/15 (Matthew McVay), 15 (Rich Fishman), 21 bottom (Jon Riley), 27 Greg Pease. **The Stock Market Photo Agency Inc.:** pages 6, 24 (Lester Lefkowitz), 29 top (Zefa/Joe Sohm). **Ecoscene:** cover top (Wayne Lawler) and pages 1 (Jim Winkley), 4-5 (Nick Hawkes), 5 (Erik Schaffer), 10 (Ian Harwood), 13 bottom (Bruce Harber), 19 top (Wayne Lawler), 26 (John Farmer), 28 (Jim Winkley), 29 bottom (Kevin King). **Panos Pictures:** pages 14 (Chris Stowers), 17 bottom (David Reed), 18 (Arabella Cecil), 22 (Chris Stowers), 25 top & 26-27 (Jim Holmes). **Environmental Picture Library:** pages 7 (Irene Lengui). **Environmental Images:** 17 top (Martin Bond). **Still Pictures:** pages 11 bottom (Matt Meadows), 19 bottom (Mark Edwards), 20 (Peter Frischmuth), 21top (Nick Cobbing), 23 top (Dylan Garcia), 25 bottom (Mark Edwards). **Science Photo Library:** 9 top (Simon Fraser), 11 top (Martin Bond). **Corbis Images:** page 23 bottom (Neil Beer).

Artwork: Raymond Turvey.

EARTH WATCH: WASTE DISPOSAL was produced for Franklin
       Watts by Bender Richardson White.
Project Editor: Lionel Bender
Text Editor: Clare Oliver
Designer: Ben White
Picture Researchers: Cathy Stastny and Daniela Marceddu
Media Conversion and Make-up: Mike Weintroub,
       MW Graphics, and Clare Oliver
Cover Make-up: Mike Pilley, Pelican Graphics
Production: Kim Richardson

For Franklin Watts:
Series Editor: Sarah Snashall
Art Director: Jonathan Hair
Cover Design: Jason Anscomb

First published in 2000 by Franklin Watts

First American edition 2000 by Franklin Watts
A Division of Grolier Publishing
90 Sherman Turnpike
Danbury, CT 06816

Visit Franklin Watts on the Internet at
http//publishing.grolier.com

Library of Congress Cataloging-in-Publication Data
Morgan, Sally
   Waste disposal/Sally Morgan
        p. cm --(Earthwatch)
   Includes index.
   Summary: Examines the different kinds of waste, from household
trash to industrial waste, describing where it goes and how it affects
the environment.
   ISBN 0-531-14557-3
   1. Refuse and refuse disposal--Juvenile literature. 2. Factory and trade
waste--Juvenile literature. 3. Recycling (Waste, etc.)--Juvenile literature.
[1. Water supply.] I. Title. II Series.

TD792.M67 1999
628.4'4--dc21   99-053857

CONTENTS

ALL OUR WASTE

Each day, everybody throws something away. A chocolate bar is eaten and the wrapper thrown away. A newspaper is read and discarded. This all adds up to mountains of waste, including paper, plastic, metals, and glass.

Waste from Homes and Offices

Trash from our homes and litter in the streets are just a tiny part of the garbage produced each year. Shops, schools, offices, and hospitals all produce garbage and dirty water, too.

Wastewater gushes from this rusty old pipe straight into the sea.

Waste from Industry

Power stations and chemical plants produce waste gases, while mines produce huge spoil heaps. There is waste, too, from farming when farmers grow crops or keep animals. A lot of this waste can be harmful to the environment if it is not disposed of carefully.

Using Resources Wisely

There are only so many natural resources, or raw materials, on the planet. People are wasting these resources by not using them carefully. We have to learn how to make good use of resources. One way forward is to recycle or reuse as much of our waste as possible. This helps reduce environmental damage and saves resources.

At this power station, coal is burned to create energy to make electricity. This process produces waste gases and steam that are released into the atmosphere.

Household waste must be collected regularly or it will mount up, as it has here in southern Spain. This pile is a week's waste from twenty houses.

EVERYDAY WASTE

In the developed world, people have their garbage collected. Each week, a family of four throws away at least a whole trash can full of waste.

Garbage Bins

It is easy to put refuse, or garbage, in a bin. A garbage collector empties the bin, now ready for you to fill it up again.

The amount of garbage people produce is increasing. This is mainly because more and more packaging material is used to protect items we buy. The bulk of garbage we throw away is paper, cardboard, and garden-plant waste. Much of this could be recycled.

Some people do not make the effort to take their garbage to dumps. Littering the countryside ruins its beauty and can be harmful to local wildlife.

Valuable Garbage

Much of what we throw away is valuable. In developing countries, many people cannot afford to throw away plastic bags and bottles—things we take for granted. The poorest people pick through garbage, sorting out valuable materials that can be sold for recycling. They sell unwanted metal and plastic so other people can reuse it. Where wood is in short supply, people use old tires, bottles, and cans as building materials.

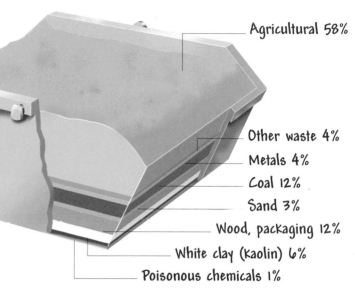

INDUSTRIAL GARBAGE THROWN AWAY

- Agricultural 58%
- Other waste 4%
- Metals 4%
- Coal 12%
- Sand 3%
- Wood, packaging 12%
- White clay (kaolin) 6%
- Poisonous chemicals 1%

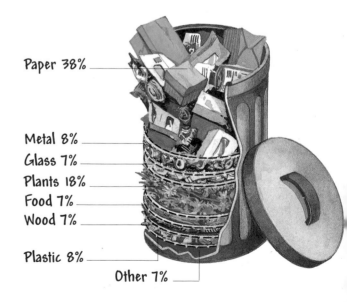

HOUSEHOLD GARBAGE THROWN AWAY

- Paper 38%
- Metal 8%
- Glass 7%
- Plants 18%
- Food 7%
- Wood 7%
- Plastic 8%
- Other 7%

In Manila, capital city of the Philippines, people search through a garbage dump. They use the materials they find to build shacks, called barong barongs.

HOLES IN THE GROUND

Do you know where your garbage is taken? In many countries, garbage is taken to huge holes in the ground that were once quarries or gravel pits. These holes are called landfill sites.

A tanker pours its load of liquid waste into a landfill.

Filling the Hole

Garbage is very bulky, so it is sometimes squashed at a refuse center before it reaches the landfill. In other places, bulldozers flatten the garbage on-site. Each week, the garbage is covered by a layer of soil. When the landfill is full, one last, thick layer of soil is scattered on top. Eventually, the land can be used for farming, housing, or industry.

Eco Thought

In many countries, huge amounts of disposable diapers are crowding landfills. The diapers produce a lot of methane gas and take centuries to break down. It is more environmentally friendly to use cloth diapers, which can be washed and reused.

Landfill Problems

Landfills are a cheap way of disposing of large amounts of garbage. But there are problems. The sites tend to be smelly and unattractive. The garbage attracts disease-carrying pests such as mice, rats, and birds. High winds can blow litter onto the surrounding land. Sometimes, poisonous chemicals leak into the soil and water supplies. To prevent this leakage, new landfill sites have to have special plastic liners.

At this landfill site near Bilbao, Spain, plastic sheeting will stop poisons from being washed into the soil once the site is filled.

A bulldozer piles up household waste at a landfill site. Birds feed on food scraps at the site. Ninety percent of the world's waste ends up in landfill sites.

Free Gas Supply

Most of the garbage in the landfill decays, or rots, over some weeks or months. As it does so, it releases a gas called methane. There is a risk of explosion if the gas is allowed to build up underground, so pipes carry the methane to the surface, where it escapes into the air. Sometimes the gas is burned on-site. Methane can also be collected and used as fuel. At some landfills, it is piped to local factories where it is burned in boilers to produce heat.

WASTE TO ENERGY

As landfill sites fill up, people have to find alternative ways of getting rid of their garbage. One way is to burn the garbage in special ovens called incinerators.

Burning Garbage

Garbage is made up of materials that release energy when they are burned, such as paper and plastic. This means that garbage can be used as a fuel. First, the garbage is sorted so that all the valuable and recyclable material is removed—for example, metal and glass. Then the rest of the waste can be burned in the incinerator.

A sorting machine, called a rotary screen, automatically separates out the different kinds of garbage.

Eco Thought
One garbage can full of ordinary household garbage can generate as much electricity as a bag of coal.

Heating Up

The temperature inside the incinerator needs to reach about 1,830°F (1,000 °C). If the temperature is too low, poisonous fumes can pollute the air. The heat energy given off by the burning garbage is used to generate electricity or to heat local homes and businesses. The small amount of waste left in the ovens can be used as a filler in road building.

Some of the huge amounts of garbage can be compressed into little blocks known as refuse derived fuel (RDF) pellets. These pellets are sold as a fuel for burning on fires and in boilers.

RDF pellets, made from domestic garbage, can be burned to provide power or heat.

Producing Biogas

The rotting wastes in landfill sites produce methane gas. On a much smaller scale, methane can be produced from human, animal, and food wastes. The organic wastes are dumped in an underground pit, where they decay. As they do this, they release gases, including methane gas, just as in landfill sites. This gas, called biogas, can be piped to homes to be used as a fuel for heating water and cooking.

On the Ground

Farm animals produce a lot of waste in the form of droppings and manure. Some of this can be composted and used as a natural fertilizer on the fields. Animal waste can also be dried and burned in special power stations to produce electricity. This way, farm waste becomes a useful fuel.

At this power plant in the United States, garbage is squashed and stored prior to being burned in an incinerator.

WASTE FROM ENERGY

Electricity is an essential part of our lives. We use it to power appliances such as lights, televisions, and computers. But electricity production creates various types of waste.

Generating Electricity

Electricity is produced in power stations. Many power stations burn fossil fuels such as coal, gas, and oil, which release heat energy. The burning fuels produce gases such as carbon dioxide and sulfur dioxide. Carbon dioxide is a greenhouse gas and adds to global warming. Sulfur dioxide produces acid rain, which damages trees and buildings.

At fossil fuel power stations, like this one in the province of Ontario, Canada, heat is used to boil water to produce steam. The steam spins wheels called turbines, which help generate electricity.

Cleaner Power

Modern power stations have special chimney filters that absorb the sulfur dioxide. This way, the waste gases from the chimney are much cleaner. Air pollution can also be reduced by burning cleaner fuels, such as natural gas, instead of coal. There is a limited supply of fossil fuels. In the long run, it will be much better to switch to cleaner, renewable sources of energy such as solar and wind power, which produce hardly any waste.

This coal mine supplies the power station (on the skyline) with coal. It also creates large amounts of waste rock containing chemicals that are washed away by rain, polluting the environment.

Eco Thought

The limestone filters in power station chimneys have to be replaced regularly, which creates lots of limestone waste. This waste is a good fertilizer. Each year, power stations in the United States produce 100 million tons of limestone waste, enough to fertilize up to 25 percent of the country's farmland.

At this Danish power station, a limestone filter in the chimney stops sulfur dioxide from escaping into the atmosphere.

NUCLEAR WASTE

Nuclear power stations produce electricity without creating air pollution. They are powered by a metal called uranium, which releases much more energy than the same amount of fossil fuel does.

Radioactive Materials

Inside a nuclear power station, rods of uranium are lowered into a reactor, where tiny particles called neutrons are fired at them. The uranium atoms split, releasing heat energy—and dangerous, radioactive particles. These contaminate all the materials inside the reactor as well as solid and liquid wastes formed during the reaction. Radioactive materials are harmful to all living things, including humans. Some of them remain harmful for centuries.

Eco Thought
The old fuel rods and reactor parts are highly radioactive, so they are placed in steel containers and surrounded by concrete. They have to be buried deep underground for hundreds, or even thousands, of years.

Nuclear power stations have safety devices to make sure that radioactive materials do not escape into the environment —even small leaks of radioactive water can be harmful and long lasting. They also have to dispose of the nuclear waste.

On Lanyu Island, Taiwan, nuclear waste is securely stored in concrete bunkers.

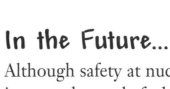

In the Future...

Although safety at nuclear power stations has improved, people feel much safer without them. In Europe and North America, old nuclear power stations have been shut down. At the same time, scientists are working on safer ways of producing nuclear power, using water and hydrogen.

Environmental workers use special equipment to check drums of radioactive waste for leaks.

Slightly radioactive waste is stored in drums and buried in pits, like this one at Hanford, Washington.

Eco Thought

The world's worst nuclear accident was at Chernobyl, Ukraine, in 1986. An explosion there produced a radioactive cloud that spread across Europe. Radioactive rain fell in Scandinavia and Britain, contaminating grasslands and affecting millions of sheep.

DIRTY WATER

Many factories use water. Some of them are built by rivers or on the coast where they can get a good supply of water. Farmers need water to irrigate their crops. Once factories and farmers have used the water, they empty it into rivers and seas.

Waste from mines

Sources of river pollution include wastewater from factories, mines, and power stations. Fertilizers and domestic sewage also pollute river water.

Warm water from power stations

Waste from factories

Fertilizers from farms

Thermal Pollution

Power stations use cold water to cool the steam. Many other industries use water for cooling, too. When it is finished with, the water is warm, and is emptied into rivers or back into the sea. Warm water contains much less oxygen than cold water. This means that aquatic life, especially fish, cannot get enough oxygen to survive. Adding warm water to rivers and seas is called thermal pollution.

Domestic sewage

Harmful Wastes

Industrial and farm wastes, sewage, and slurry (thick liquid wastes) are emptied into rivers and seas. Some waste contains poisons, such as pesticides and oil. Bacteria in the water feed on sewage and slurry. As they feed, they use up oxygen, so the water cannot support much other life.

Killer Weed

Fertilizers and sewage contain nutrients that encourage the growth of tiny plants called algae. As the algae multiply, they cover the surface of the river like a blanket, blocking sunlight from the plants below and causing them to die.

Filthy foam washed up on the beach is a tell-tale sign that this seawater is polluted.

Stopping Pollution

In developed countries, there are strict laws controlling water quality. Environmental agencies sample the water, and they can fine companies that pollute it. Dirty rivers and polluted beaches are becoming a thing of the past. Unfortunately, it is much more difficult to monitor seawater and to prevent people from dumping waste far out at sea.

A huge tanker is loaded with nuclear waste to be dumped at sea.

TOXIC WASTE

Toxic, or poisonous, chemicals are harmful to living organisms. Some toxic chemicals have important uses, especially in medicine and industry, while others are produced as waste products of chemical processes.

Buried in the Ground

In the past, toxic chemicals were just buried in the ground. No one bothered to record where the waste was buried. Some housing developments were built on the toxic sites, and now they have to be torn down. It is unsafe for people to live there because toxic chemicals have contaminated the soil and leaked into the water supply.

Eco Thought

Beluga whales are found in the Great Lakes and the St. Lawrence River in the United States. Heavy industry has polluted the water with toxic chemicals. The belugas feed on fish that have eaten contaminated plankton. When dead whales wash up on the shores, they have to be treated as toxic waste because their bodies contain such high levels of pollutants.

This Bolivian mine has closed, but toxic chemicals from the mine continue to pollute the river.

There are only traces of toxic pesticides in these discarded containers, but that is enough to contaminate the water supply.

Long-Lasting Problem

The Hudson River in New York State has been polluted by chemicals called PCBs for more than 100 years. PCBs were once used in power stations, but were found to be poisonous. They are still leaking into the river from old and abandoned industrial sites, contaminating the fish. The only way to clean up the river is to remove tons of mud and slime from the riverbed.

Making It Safe

The easiest way to clean up a toxic waste site is to remove all the contaminated soil. But what happens to the soil? Some plants will take up the chemicals through their roots, and then the plants can be burned. Water containing toxic chemicals can be treated with ultraviolet (U.V.) light. The strong light breaks down the chemicals into safe substances.

Scientists take water samples from the River Weaver in northwest England. They will test the water regularly for poisons and oxygen content.

Recycling Waste

Much of the garbage we throw away could be used again. It could be put to a new use, or recycled and made into something new. This would help us to save resources.

These picket fences are made entirely from recycled plastic.

Reusing Building Materials

It is not just household waste that can be recycled. Industry can reuse and recycle materials, too. Building materials such as bricks, tiles, doors, and windows can be taken out of old buildings and used again in new ones. This saves digging raw materials out of quarries, cutting down trees, or making new items in factories. Many companies have programs to reduce the waste their factories produce.

This pile of garden waste has been shredded. Once it has rotted, it will make useful compost.

Taking Part

There's no need to throw away garden waste. It can either be recycled at home on a compost heap and then put back on the garden, or it can be taken to a local compost recycling center where it will be put on huge compost heaps and then sold back to the public.

Problems with Plastic

People are using increasingly large amounts of plastic. Plastic waste is increasing by ten percent each year. Recycling plastic is not a simple process because there are so many different types, and each has to be recycled separately. A single bottle can be made from three different plastics—a hard plastic for the cap; transparent, flexible plastic for the bottle; and another hard plastic for the flat bottom piece.

Manufacturers can help by using fewer plastics in each object. They can also stamp each plastic with a code to make it easier to sort them.

At a recycling center, the first job is to separate the plastic and glass so that they can be processed.

GLASS RECYCLING

Glass is a useful material and is easy to recycle. Glass windows cannot be recycled because they contain a complex mix of chemicals, but glass bottles and jars can be.

Recycling Glass

The raw materials used to make glass are sand and limestone, which are mixed and heated to 2,700°F (1,500 °C) in a furnace until they melt. The liquid glass is blown or rolled into the right shape. When glass is recycled, the different colors of glass are separated and then broken up. The broken glass, called cullet, is dumped in batches into the furnace along with the sand and limestone.

At this recycling plant in County Cork, Ireland, bottles are sorted and then sent back to the manufacturers to be reused.

In a glass recycling plant, cullet made from bottles of the same color is heaped in piles ready to be loaded into the furnace.

Reusing Bottles

Even more money can be saved if bottles are reused. Milk and soft drink bottles, for example, can be collected and taken back to the manufacturer, who washes them and fills them again. Often it is possible to reuse a bottle many times before it needs to be recycled.

Saving Materials

Recycling glass means that less sand and limestone have to be quarried to make new glass. Also, cullet melts at a lower temperature than do sand and limestone, so the furnace does not need to be as hot, and this saves energy. However, the cost of transporting the collected glass for recycling can be greater than that of bringing raw materials from quarries to the glass factories.

At this bottling plant in Mexico, most of the drink bottles are made from recycled glass.

On the Ground

In parts of Europe, Australia, and North America, local councils collect recyclable items from homes. Residents must separate glassware from other waste, and this is collected by vans each week. For each ton of glass, recycling instead of making new glass saves 36 gallons (136 liters) of fuel oil.

RECYCLING METALS

Many metals exist in the ground as ores—mixtures of metal and other materials. Each ore has to be dug from the ground and treated to extract the metal. This process uses up a lot of energy and leaves behind a lot of waste rock.

This pile of scrap metal is being left to rust. It could be melted down and reused instead.

Melt Down

Recycling metals saves resources and reduces the need to dig new ore from the ground. Therefore, recycling produces less waste. Also, some metals, such as gold, silver, and titanium, are in short supply so are too valuable to throw away.

Eco Thought

It takes 20 times more energy to make an aluminum can from bauxite than from an old aluminum can. As much as half of the aluminum in a drink can has probably been recycled.

An All-Purpose Metal

Aluminum is made from an ore called bauxite. In countries such as Australia and Ghana, bauxite is quarried from the ground and transported to aluminum smelters, where it is crushed and heated so that the metal can be extracted. Aluminum is a light, but strong, metal that is ideal for making cooking foil and garden furniture.

This man chops up cans to separate tin from aluminum.

Taking Part

Aluminum needs to be separated from iron and steel for recycling. Use a magnet to distinguish between the metal of drink cans. Iron and steel are magnetic, so a magnet will stick to them. Magnets do not stick to aluminum as it is not magnetic.

In Western Australia, tropical forests are cleared to make way for a bauxite quarry.

Fewer Quarries

Most drink cans are made from metals such as aluminum and steel. The average person in the United States uses 130 drink cans a year. As more aluminum is used, more bauxite has to be quarried. Often, tropical rain forests are cleared to make way for the quarries.

By recycling aluminum, the rain forests can be saved. Less oil is needed to transport the bauxite to the smelter, and less energy is needed to extract the metal. If we repeatedly recycled all the aluminum and other metals we used, we would need far fewer new supplies.

PAPER RECYCLING

Wood is the main ingredient of paper. Most of the wood we use comes from conifer trees that are grown as a renewable crop. New paper can also be made from recycled paper. Nowadays, most developed countries recycle more than half their paper.

Making Paper

Timber is taken to a pulp mill where it is reduced to a sawdust-like pulp. The pulp is transported to a paper mill where it is mixed with water and chemicals. The mixture is spread out and the wastewater drains away, leaving a thin sheet of paper. Recycled paper is made the same way, except that pulped wastepaper replaces some or all of the wood pulp.

Good-quality paper is made from long fibers of wood. During recycling, the fibers get shorter and this reduces the quality. Even so, recycled paper is fine for newspapers and packaging.

Trees from this purpose-grown renewable forest are cut down to provide wood pulp.

Eco Thought

A person living in the United States uses 660 pounds (300 kilograms) of paper every year. That's twice as much as somebody living in the United Kingdom and 100 times more than a person living in India.

This truck in Seoul, South Korea, takes wastepaper from collection points to a recycling plant.

Saving Energy

Recycling paper conserves energy and resources and does not produce any waste timber. Energy is needed to cut down the trees, to transport the logs, to chop them up, and to pulp them. Still more energy is used to transport the pulp to the paper mill, where it will be made into paper.

Fewer Plantations

Recycling paper does not really save trees. Most wood pulp comes from fast-growing conifers or eucalyptus that are grown in plantations. However, conifer plantations are not particularly attractive, and they do not support as much wildlife as natural woodland. New plantations are being established on land that was once grassland or peat bogs, too. Recycling paper reduces the need to destroy these natural wildlife habitats.

Taking Part

Collect different types of paper such as quality writing paper, newspaper, cardboard, and recycled papers. Tear off a piece of paper and examine the edge with a magnifying glass. Can you see the fibers? How long are they? Which paper has the longest fibers?

At a paper mill, paper is produced in giant rolls called reams.

WHAT CAN WE DO?

There are all sorts of ways that you can help when dealing with waste. Just remember these three words: reduce, reuse, and recycle.

These children are putting empty glass bottles into recycling bins.

Reduce, Reuse, Recycle

First, try to reduce the amount of waste you and your family produce. Everything you buy has used energy in some way, so only buy things you really need. Before you throw something away, think about what will happen to it. Reuse means that you try and put an item to a new use. Finally, if you cannot reuse something, try to recycle it.

Less Packaging

One way to reduce waste is not to buy items with lots of packaging. Simple packaging for food is important because it keeps it clean and fresh. But often packaging is designed to make something look good and to tempt you to buy it. Layers of fancy packaging are a waste of resources. They will only end up in the trash when you get home.

Local Recycling

Find out if there is a recycling program in your neighborhood or school. Then check through your garbage for glass, paper, metal, and plastic. Keep these items separate and take them to the nearest recycling point. Wear gloves if you are handling hazardous items.

Old Clothes for New

Old clothes can either be sold at charity shops or sent for recycling. The wool from old sweaters can be re-spun and made into new yarn. Cotton can be made into high-quality paper, and synthetic fabrics can be made into stuffing for furniture.

On Earth Day—an annual event in many countries—people are encouraged to recycle hazardous household wastes.

On a Global Scale

Around the world, governments are setting up recycling programs to conserve the resources of their countries and to cut down on the amounts of waste they produce and have to treat. They are also cooperating on treating hazardous chemicals, such as nuclear waste; reducing illegal dumping at sea; and reducing global warming.

Kitchen waste, such as vegetable peelings, can be used to make rich compost.

FACT FILE

Scrap Heap

In the United States, more than seven million cars are scrapped each year. The metal and some of the plastic can be recycled.

Tire Tale

Each year more than 250 million tires are thrown away in the United States, and a further 200 million in western Europe. The United Kingdom scraps up to 30 million tires each year. Half are put in landfills, dumped, or stockpiled. Twenty percent are retreaded, 15 percent are burned, 10 percent go to engineering projects, and 5 percent are used as boat fenders and on farms.

In the Can

In 1996, more than 32 billion steel cans were made in the United States, and more than half were recycled. About 11 billion steel cans are used in the United Kingdom each year, but only 20 percent are recycled.

Plastic Fantastic

Recycled plastic has many uses. For example, it can be used to make plant pots, fencing, and waterproof boots.

Stripped Down

In the last 20 years, supermarket packaging has become one-third lighter. This helps cut down waste and saves energy.
In some supermarkets in Germany, shoppers do not have to take home unwanted packaging. They remove it from the items they have bought and put it in special recycling bins.

Steel Appeal

Steel is the world's most recycled metal. More than 300 million tons are recycled every year— about 40 percent of total worldwide liquid steel production. This saves 200 million tons of iron ore and 90 million tons of coal. "New" steel cans usually contain about 25 percent recycled steel.

Recycled Records

Today music is recorded on CDs, not vinyl records. There are millions of unwanted records in the world, and they are being collected and melted down to make bank cards.

Gotta Lotta Bottle

In 1996, 108 million used plastic containers were recovered from household waste in the United Kingdom and recycled.

Pretty Poly

Fast-food shops put food into polystyrene containers. This type of plastic traps heat, so the food does not get cold. Once polystyrene had to be thrown away, but now polystyrene can be recycled, too.

News on Trees

In the United Kingdom, the average person uses about two trees' worth of paper each year. Most of this is as newspaper.

GLOSSARY

Acid rain Rain that contains acidic pollutants, such as sulfur dioxides, and that can damage trees and buildings or contaminate plants.

Aquatic Living in water.

Atmosphere The layer of gases around Earth.

Atom The tiniest part of any substance.

Bacteria A tiny organism, too small to see with the eye. Some bacteria cause disease.

Bauxite The ore that contains aluminum.

Biogas A gas given off by plant and animal wastes as they rot.

Compress To make very small.

Conifer An evergreen tree that has needle-like leaves and bears cones instead of flowers. Most conifers grow quickly.

Contaminate To make dirty.

Cullet Broken glass.

Exhaust Waste gases pumped out by engines and chimneys of power stations and factories.

Fertilizer Nutrients added to the soil to help plant growth.

Fossil fuel Fuels, such as coal, oil, and natural gas, that have been made from the bodies of plants and animals that died millions of years ago.

Furnace A very hot oven for melting metal-containing rocks such as iron ore or the raw materials of glass.

Global warming The build up of greenhouse gases in the atmosphere that is causing Earth's temperature to rise.

Greenhouse gas Gas that traps heat in the atmosphere and keeps Earth warm.

Incinerator A large oven or furnace for burning garbage.

Landfill A large hole in the ground where garbage is buried.

Magnet A piece of iron that attracts iron and steel and, if hung on a thread, points North and South.

Neutron A particle found in the nucleus, or center, of an atom.

Nutrient Chemical that is needed for the healthy growth of plants and animals.

Pesticide Substance that will kill insect pests such as greenflies.

Plankton Microscopic plant or animal life.

Plantation A large area where crops or trees are grown.

Pollute To poison the air, water, or land.

Polystyrene Lightweight, but rigid, plastic used for packaging.

Radioactive Giving off dangerous radiation.

RDF pellet A little block of fuel made from compressed garbage.

Renewable Can be replaced.

Resources The raw materials— for example, wood, oil, gold— that are used to make things.

Slurry Thick liquid waste.

Smelter Place where ore, such as bauxite, is crushed and heated to extract metal, such as aluminum.

Spoil heap Piles of soil and waste rock dug from coal mines or quarries.

Synthetic Made by people.

Toxic Poisonous.

Ultraviolet An invisible part of sunlight.

INDEX